PIANO DUET PLAY·ALONG VOLUME 5

DISNEY FAVORITES

PLAYBACK+
Speed • Pitch • Balance • Loop

To access audio, visit:
www.halleonard.com/mylibrary

Enter Code
7155-1824-3443-5283

ISBN 978-1-4234-2130-6

Disney and Disney/Pixar characters and artwork © Disney Enterprises, Inc.

Walt Disney Music Company
Wonderland Music Company, Inc.

DISTRIBUTED BY

HAL•LEONARD®
7777 W. BLUEMOUND RD. P.O. BOX 13819 MILWAUKEE, WI 53213

In Australia Contact:
Hal Leonard Australia Pty. Ltd.
4 Lentara Court
Cheltenham, Victoria, 3192 Australia
Email: ausadmin@halleonard.com

Visit Hal Leonard Online at
www.halleonard.com

BIBBIDI-BOBBIDI-BOO
(The Magic Song)
from Walt Disney's CINDERELLA

SECONDO

Words by JERRY LIVINGSTON
Music by MACK DAVID and AL HOFFMAN

Brightly (♩ = 120)

BIBBIDI-BOBBIDI-BOO
(The Magic Song)
from Walt Disney's CINDERELLA

PRIMO

Words by JERRY LIVINGSTON
Music by MACK DAVID and AL HOFFMAN

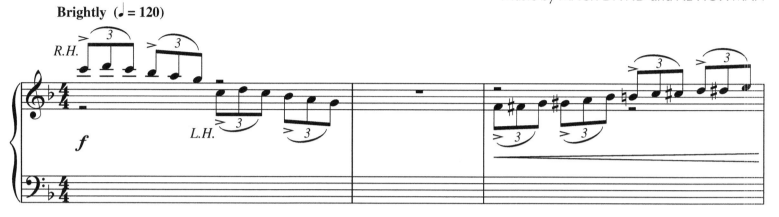

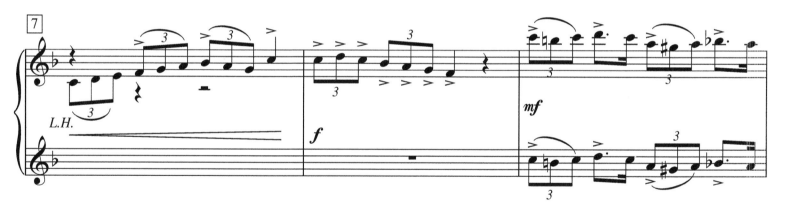

CAN YOU FEEL THE LOVE TONIGHT

from Walt Disney Pictures' THE LION KING

SECONDO

Music by ELTON JOHN
Lyrics by TIM RICE

Slowly and expressively

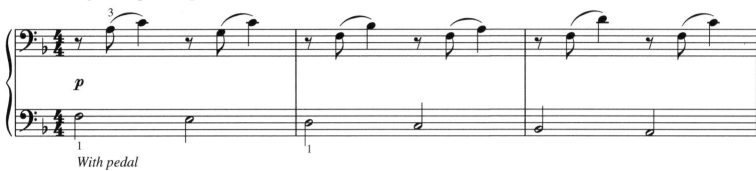

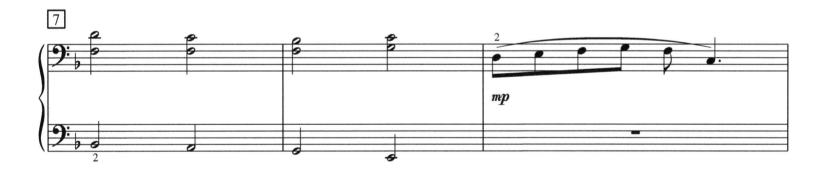

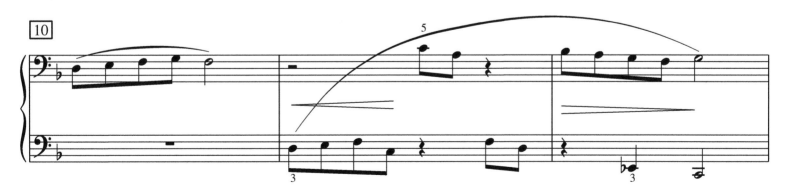

CAN YOU FEEL THE LOVE TONIGHT

from Walt Disney Pictures' THE LION KING

PRIMO

Music by ELTON JOHN
Lyrics by TIM RICE

Slowly and expressively

SECONDO

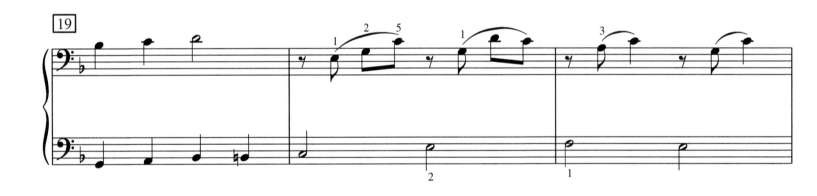

PRIMO

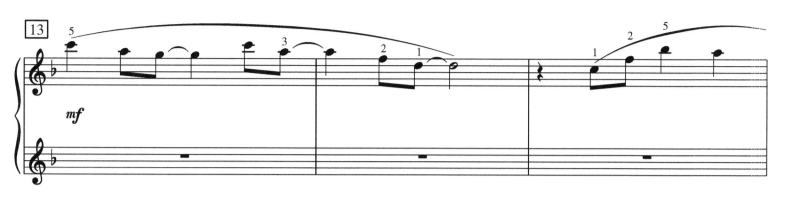

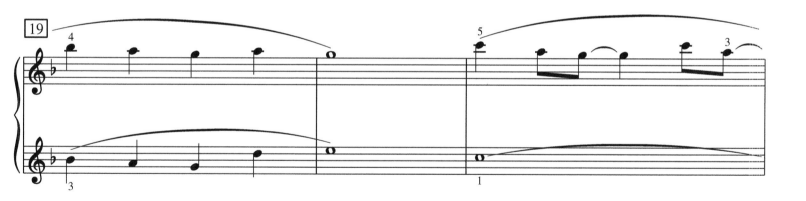

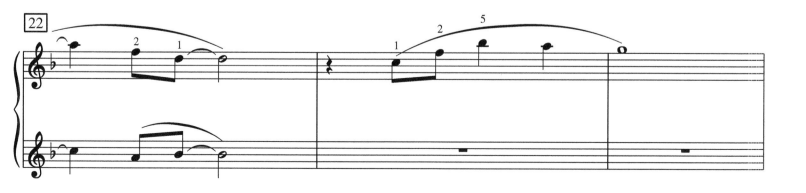

SECONDO

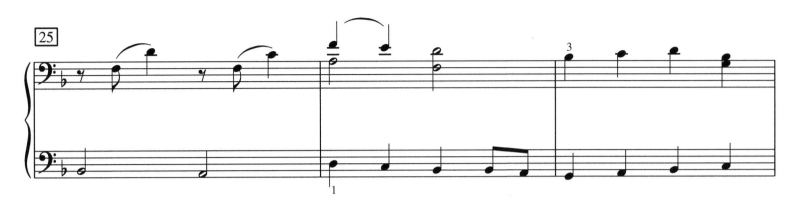

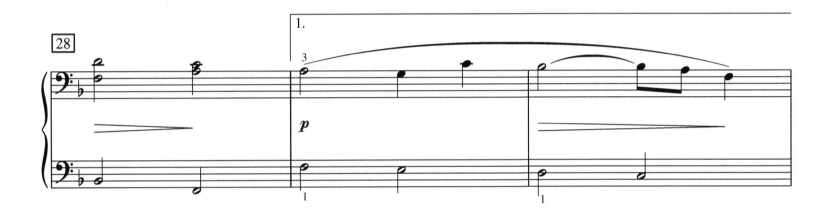

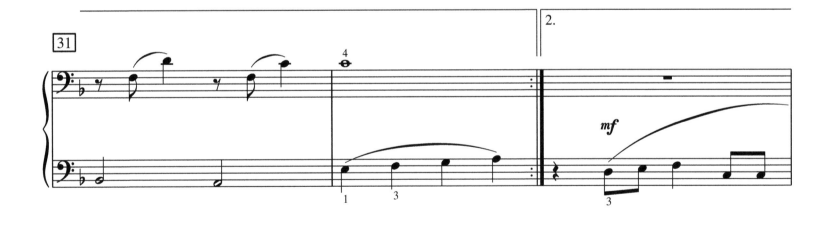

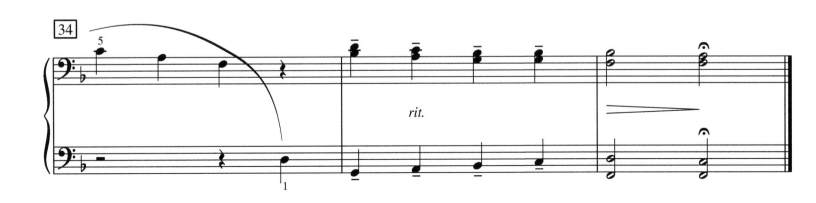

PRIMO

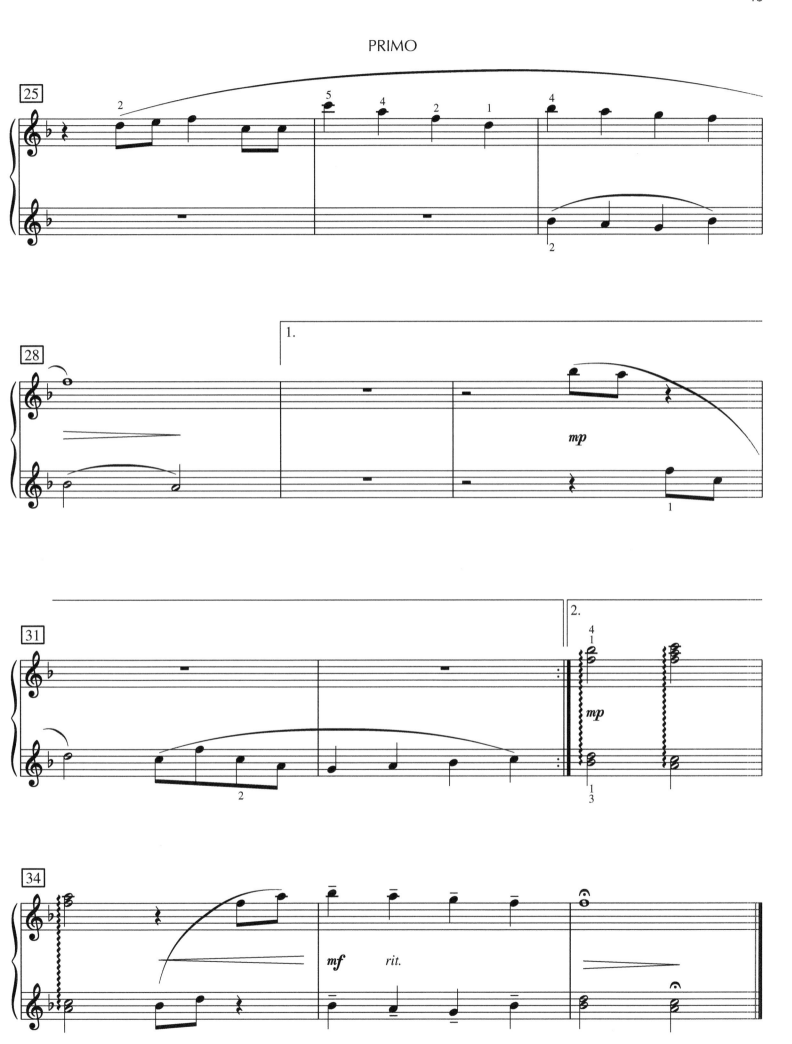

A DREAM IS A WISH YOUR HEART MAKES

from Walt Disney's CINDERELLA

SECONDO

Words and Music by MACK DAVID,
AL HOFFMAN and JERRY LIVINGSTON

Slowly and gently

A DREAM IS A WISH YOUR HEART MAKES

from Walt Disney's CINDERELLA

PRIMO

Words and Music by MACK DAVID,
AL HOFFMAN and JERRY LIVINGSTON

Slowly and gently

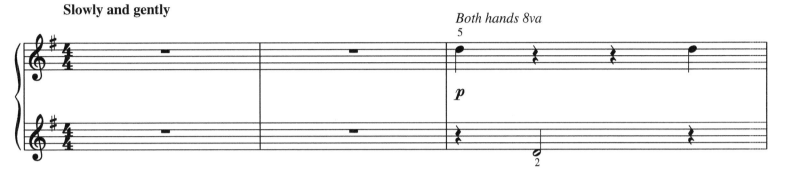

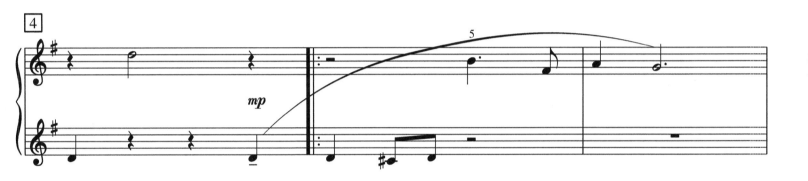

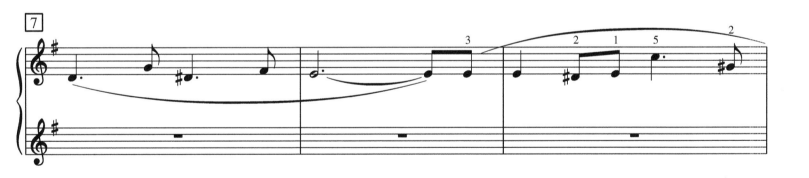

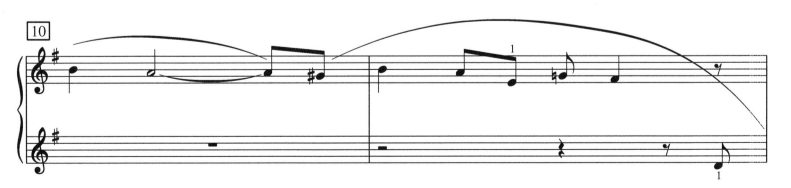

SECONDO

PRIMO

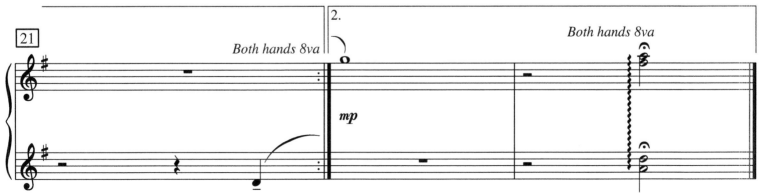

HAKUNA MATATA
from Walt Disney Pictures' THE LION KING

SECONDO

Music by ELTON JOHN
Lyrics by TIM RICE

HAKUNA MATATA
from Walt Disney Pictures' THE LION KING
PRIMO

Music by ELTON JOHN
Lyrics by TIM RICE

Slowly

Both hands 8va throughout

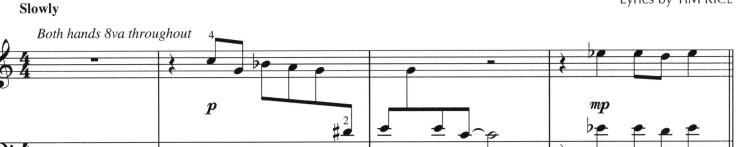

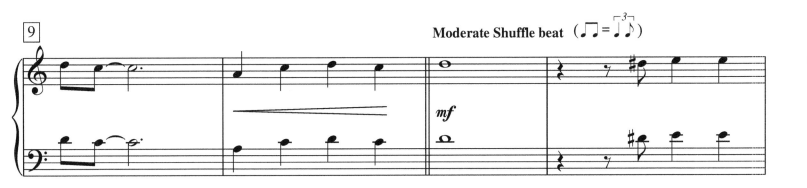

Moderate Shuffle beat

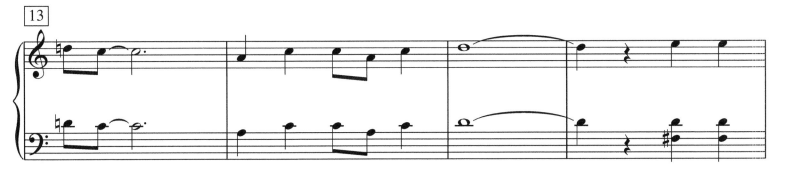

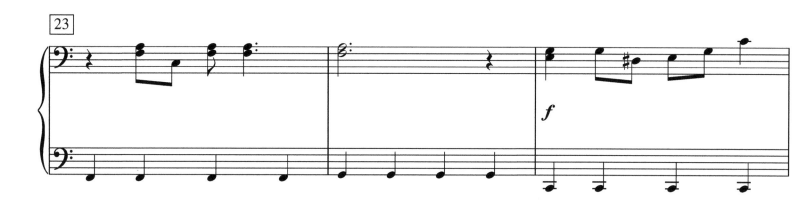

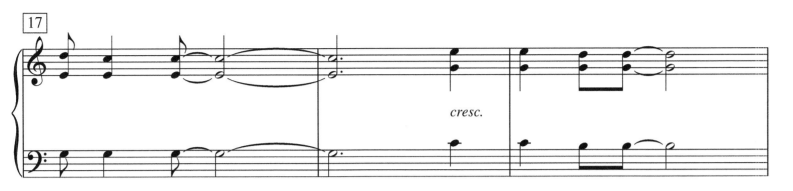

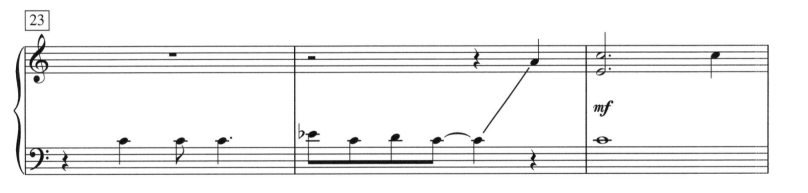

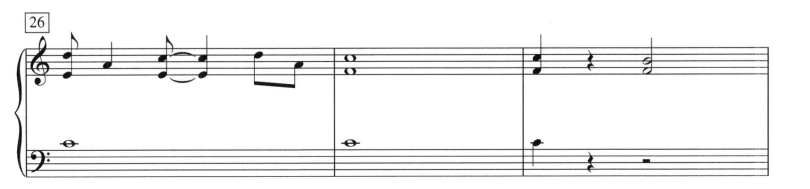

SECONDO

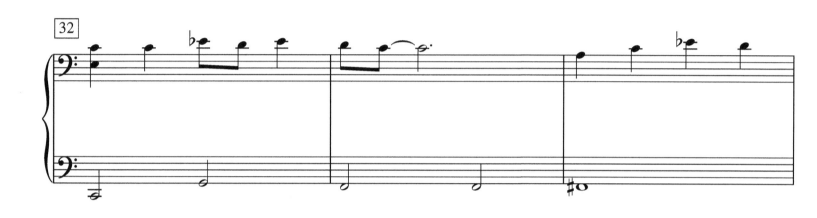

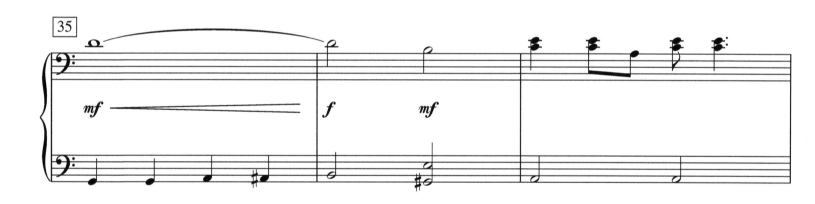

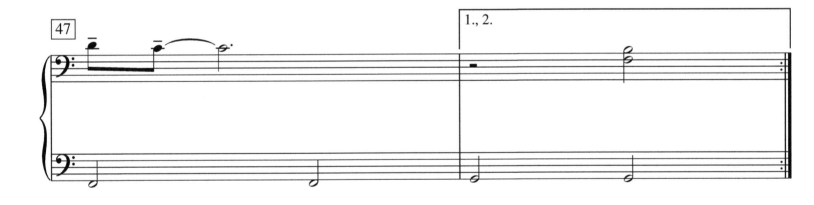

PRIMO

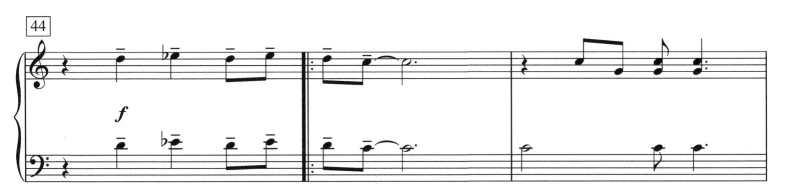

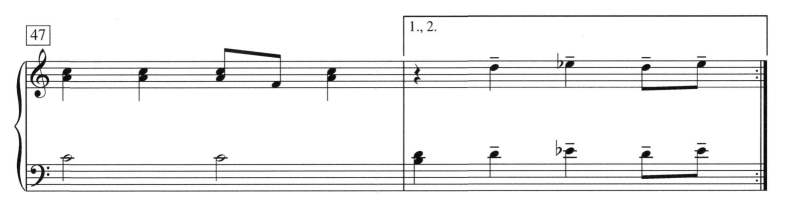

REFLECTION
from Walt Disney Pictures' MULAN

SECONDO

Music by MATTHEW WILDER
Lyrics by DAVID ZIPPEL

Slowly, with expression

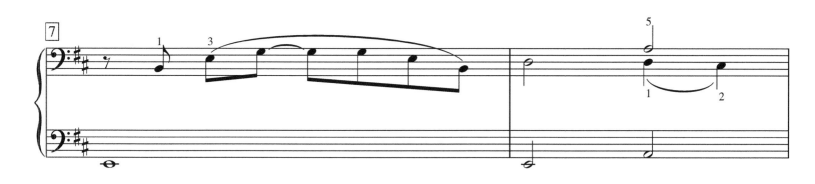

REFLECTION
from Walt Disney Pictures' MULAN

PRIMO

Music by MATTHEW WILDER
Lyrics by DAVID ZIPPEL

Slowly, with expression

SOMEDAY
from Walt Disney's THE HUNCHBACK OF NOTRE DAME

SECONDO

Music by ALAN MENKEN
Lyrics by STEPHEN SCHWARTZ

Gently

SOMEDAY
from Walt Disney's THE HUNCHBACK OF NOTRE DAME

PRIMO

Music by ALAN MENKEN
Lyrics by STEPHEN SCHWARTZ

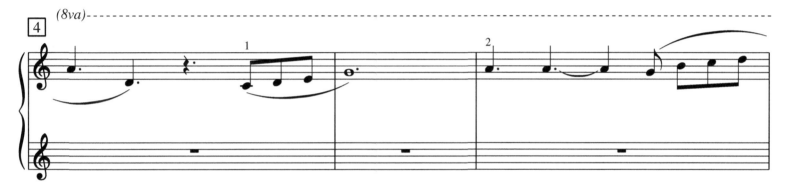

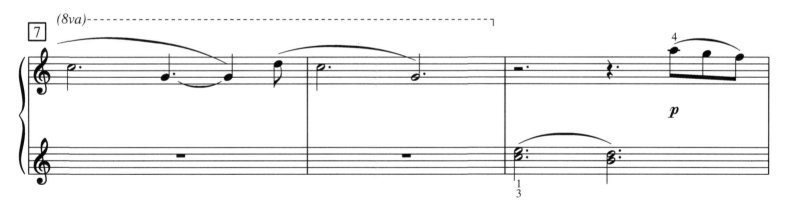

SECONDO

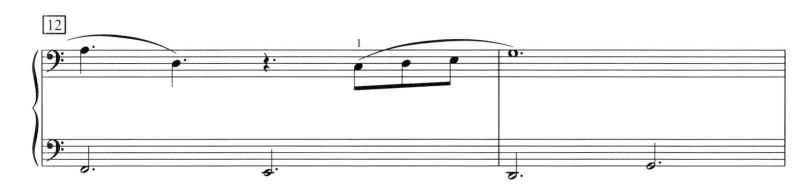

PRIMO

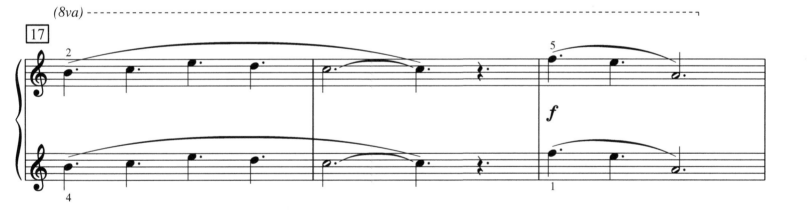

A SPOONFUL OF SUGAR

from Walt Disney's MARY POPPINS

SECONDO

Words and Music by RICHARD M. SHERMAN
and ROBERT B. SHERMAN

Brightly

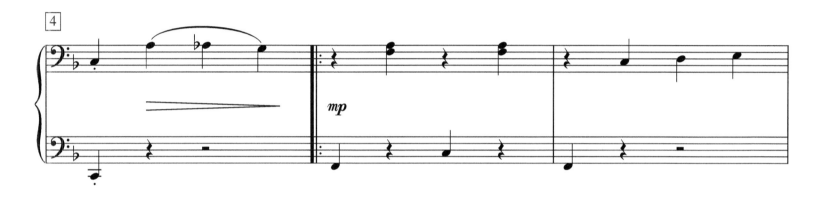

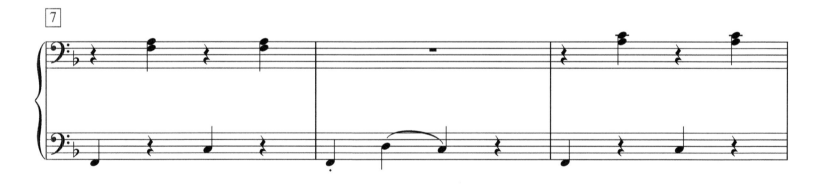

A SPOONFUL OF SUGAR

from Walt Disney's MARY POPPINS

PRIMO

Words and Music by RICHARD M. SHERMAN
and ROBERT B. SHERMAN

Brightly

Both hands 8va throughout

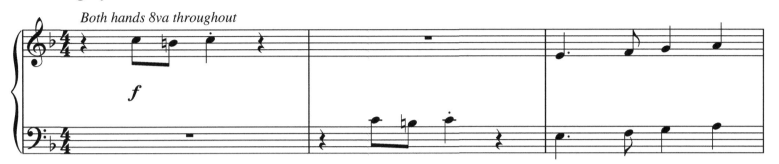

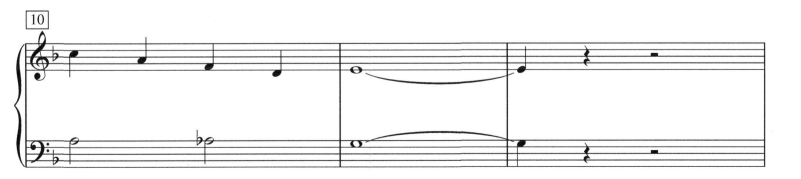

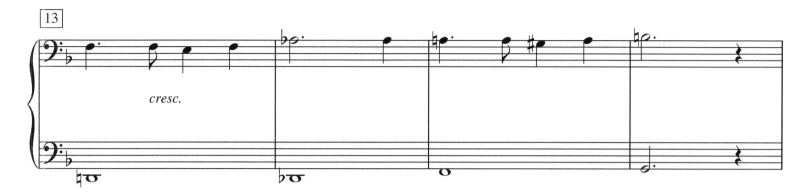

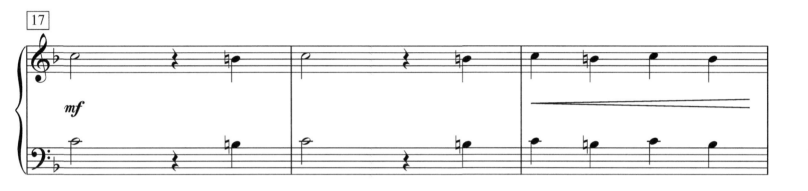

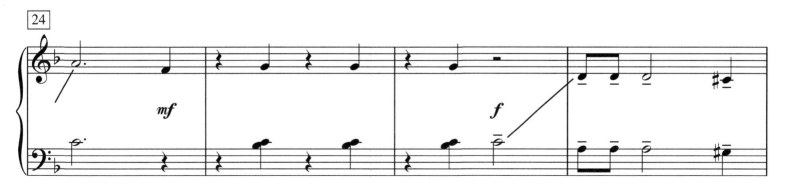

SECONDO

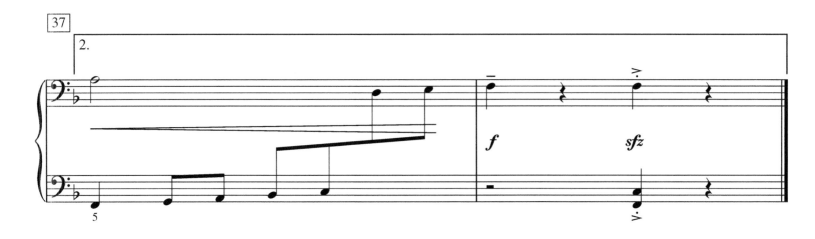

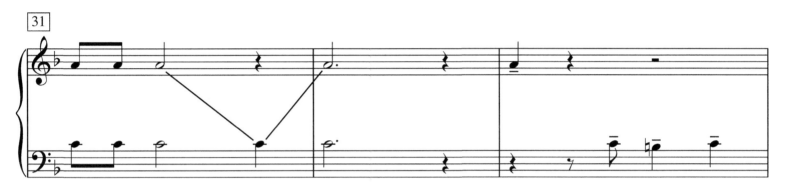

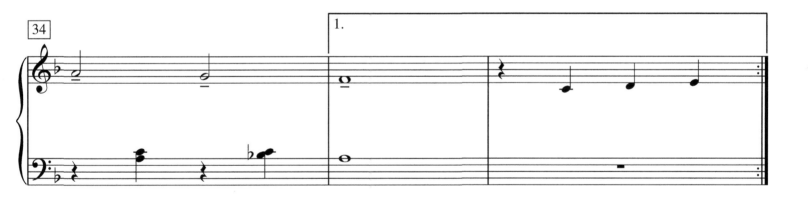

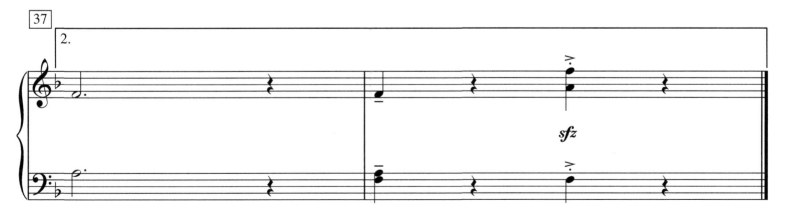

YOU'VE GOT A FRIEND IN ME

from Walt Disney's TOY STORY and TOY STORY 2

SECONDO

Music and Lyrics by
RANDY NEWMAN

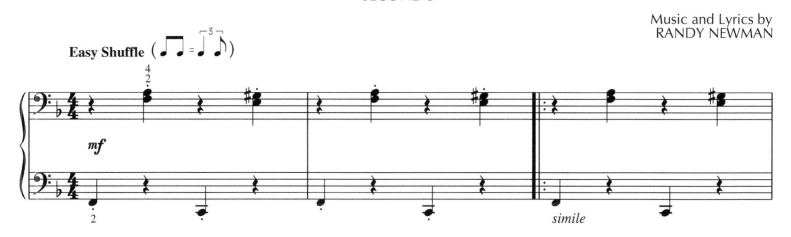

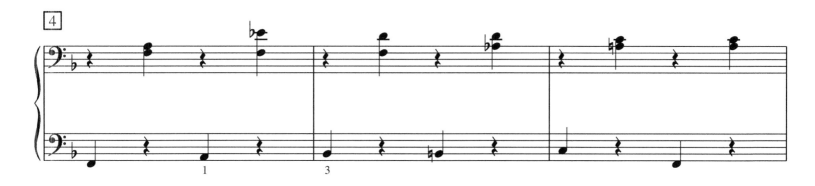

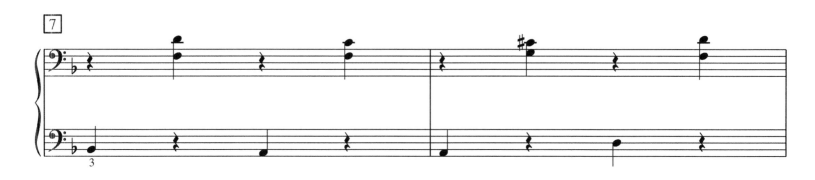

YOU'VE GOT A FRIEND IN ME

from Walt Disney's TOY STORY and TOY STORY 2

PRIMO

Music and Lyrics by
RANDY NEWMAN

SECONDO

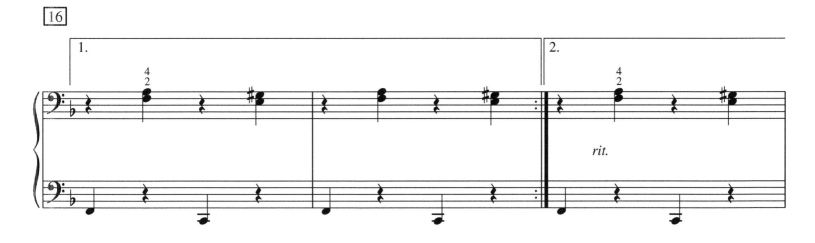

PRIMO

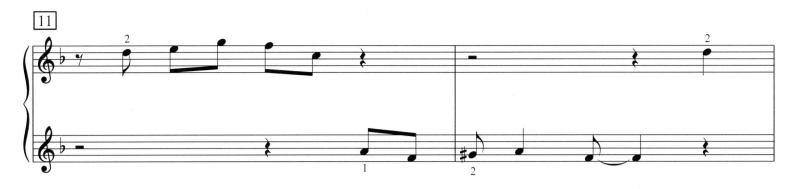

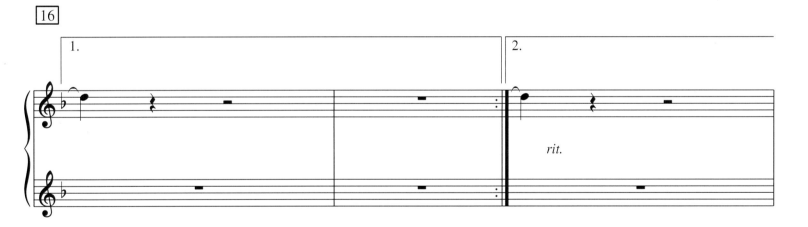

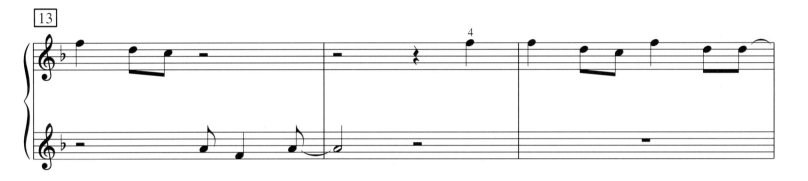

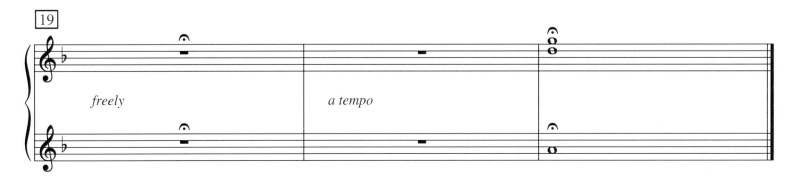

PIANO FOR TWO
A Variety of Piano Duets from Hal Leonard

ADELE FOR PIANO DUET
Intermediate Level

Eight of Adele's biggest hits arranged especially for intermediate piano duet! Featuring: Chasing Pavements • Hello • Make You Feel My Love • Rolling in the Deep • Set Fire to the Rain • Skyfall • Someone Like You • When We Were Young.
00172162 1 Piano, 4 Hands................................$14.99

THE BEATLES FOR PIANO DUET
Intermediate Level
arr. Eric Baumgartner

Eight great Beatles' songs arranged for piano duet! Titles: Blackbird • Come Together • In My Life • Lucy in the Sky with Diamonds • Michelle • Ob-la-di, Ob-la-da • While My Guitar Gently Weeps • Yellow Submarine.
00275877 1 Piano, 4 Hands.............................$14.99

THE BIG BOOK OF PIANO DUETS

24 great piano duet arrangements! Includes: Beauty and the Beast • Clocks • Edelweiss • Georgia on My Mind • He's a Pirate • Let It Go • Linus and Lucy • Moon River • Yellow Submarine • You are the Sunshine of My Life • and more!
00232851 1 Piano, 4 Hands...............................$17.99

CONTEMPORARY DISNEY DUETS
Intermediate Level

8 great Disney duets: Evermore (from Beauty and the Beast) • How Does a Moment Last Forever (from Beauty and the Beast) • How Far I'll Go (from Moana) • Lava • Let It Go (from Frozen) • Proud Corazon (from Coco) • Remember Me (from Coco) • You're Welcome (from Moana).
00285562 1 Piano, 4 Hands............................$12.99

EASY CLASSICAL DUETS
Book/Online Audio
Willis Music

7 great piano duets to perform at a recital, play-for-fun, or sightread: By the Beautiful Blue Danube (Strauss) • Eine kleine Nachtmusik (Mozart) • Hungarian Rhapsody No. 5 (Liszt) • Morning from Peer Gynt (Grieg) • Rondeau (Mouret) • Sleeping Beauty Waltz (Tchaikovsky) • Surprise Symphony (Haydn). Includes online audio tracks for the primo and secondo part for download or streaming.
00145767 1 Piano, 4 Hands...........................$12.99

FAVORITE DISNEY SONGS FOR PIANO DUET
Early Intermediate Level

8 great Disney songs creatively arranged for piano duet: Can You Feel the Love Tonight • Do You Want to Build a Snowman • A Dream Is a Wish Your Heart Makes • Supercalifragilisticexpialidocious • That's How You Know • When Will My Life Begin? • You'll Be in My Heart • You've Got a Friend in Me.
00285563 1 Piano, 4 Hands...........................$14.99

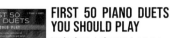

FIRST 50 PIANO DUETS YOU SHOULD PLAY

Includes: Autumn Leaves • Bridge over Troubled Water • Chopsticks • Fields of Gold • Hallelujah • Imagine • Lean on Me • Theme from "New York, New York" • Over the Rainbow • Peaceful Easy Feeling • Singin' in the Rain • A Thousand Years • What the World Needs Now Is Love • You Raise Me Up • and more.
00276571 1 Piano, 4 Hands...........................$24.99

GOSPEL DUETS
The Phillip Keveren Series

Eight inspiring hymns arranged by Phillip Keveren for one piano, four hands, including: Church in the Wildwood • His Eye Is on the Sparrow • In the Garden • Just a Closer Walk with Thee • The Old Rugged Cross • Shall We Gather at the River? • There Is Power in the Blood • When the Roll Is Called up Yonder.
00295099 1 Piano, 4 Hands...........................$12.99

THE GREATEST SHOWMAN
by Benj Pasek & Justin Paul
Intermediate Level

Creative piano duet arrangements for the songs: Come Alive • From Now On • The Greatest Show • A Million Dreams • Never Enough • The Other Side • Rewrite the Stars • This Is Me • Tightrope.
00295078 1 Piano, 4 Hands........................... $16.99

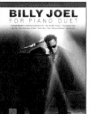

BILLY JOEL FOR PIANO DUET
Intermediate Level

8 of the Piano Man's greatest hits – perfect as recital encores, or just for fun! Titles: It's Still Rock and Roll to Me • Just the Way You Are • The Longest Time • My Life • New York State of Mind • Piano Man • She's Always a Woman • Uptown Girl.
00141139 1 Piano, 4 Hands $14.99

HEART AND SOUL & OTHER DUET FAVORITES

8 fun duets arranged for two people playing on one piano. Includes: Any Dream Will Do • Chopsticks • Heart and Soul • Music! Music! Music! (Put Another Nickel In) • On Top of Spaghetti • Raiders March • The Rainbow Connection • Y.M.C.A..
00290541 1 Piano, 4 Hands $12.99

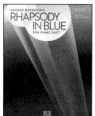

RHAPSODY IN BLUE
George Gershwin/
arr. Brent Edstrom

Originally written for piano and jazz band, "Rhapsody in Blue" was later orchestrated by Ferde Grofe. This intimate adaptation for piano duet delivers access to advancing pianists and provides an exciting musical collaboration and adventure!
00125150 1 Piano, 4 Hands $14.99

RIVER FLOWS IN YOU & OTHER SONGS FOR PIANO DUET
Intermediate Level

10 great songs including the title song and: All of Me (Piano Guys) • Bella's Lullaby • Beyond • Chariots of Fire • Dawn • Forrest Gump - Main Title (Feather Theme) • Primavera • Somewhere in Time • Watermark.
00141055 1 Piano, 4 Hands $12.99

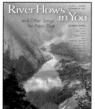

TOP HITS FOR EASY PIANO DUET
Book/Online Audio
arr. David Pearl

10 great songs with backing tracks: Despacito (Justin Bieber ft. Luis Fonsi & Daddy Yankee) • Havana (Camila Cabello ft. Young Thug • High Hopes (Panic! At the Disco) • A Million Dreams (*The Greatest Showman*) • Perfect (Ed Sheeran) • Senorita (Camila Cabello & Shawn Mendes) • Shallow (Lady Gaga & Bradley Cooper) • Someone You Loved (Lewis Capaldi) • Speechless (*Aladdin*) • Sucker (Jonas Brothers).
00326133 1 Piano, 4 Hands.............................$12.99

HAL•LEONARD®
www.halleonard.com

0722
054